See It,
Write It

Picture Yourself
writing
POETRY

Using **Photos** to **Inspire** Writing

by Laura Purdie Salas

CAPSTONE PRESS
a capstone imprint

Fact Finders are published by Capstone Press,
1710 Roe Crest Drive, North Mankato, Minnesota. 56003.
www.capstonepub.com

Library of Congress Cataloging-in-Publication Data
Salas, Laura Purdie.
  Picture yourself writing poetry : using photos to inspire writing / by Laura Purdie Salas.
  p. cm.—(Fact finders. see it, write it)
  Includes bibliographical references and index.
  Summary: "Useful tips and writing prompts show young writers how to use images to inspire poetry
writing"—Provided by publisher.
  ISBN 978-1-4296-6124-9 (library binding)
  ISBN 978-1-4296-7209-2 (paperback)
  1. Poetry—Authorship—Juvenile literature. 2. Literature and photography—Juvenile literature. I. Title.
  PN1059.A9S345 2012
  808.1—dc22   2010052356

Editorial Credits
Jennifer Besel, editor; Veronica Correia, designer; Eric Manske, production specialist

Photo Credits
Alamy: Jennie Lewis, 22; Brand X Pictures, 18; CORBIS RF, 14; CORBIS: Jeffry W. Myers, 17; Corel, 9;
Digital Vision, 8, 24; Dreamstime: Lu2006, 16, Remy Levine, 13; Gail Lewis, 32; Getty Images Inc.:
Stone/Ryan McVay, 25; iStockphoto: RonTech2000, 15; NARA , 20; Photo Researchers, Inc: Gerard
Lodriguss, 27; Shutterstock: Cathy Keifer, 7, David Lee, 23, Helen & Vlad Filatov, 3, 28, jared_medley,
26, Joshua Lewis, 21, Michiel de Wit, 10, Rufous, 19, Sam Cornwell, 11, Sebastian Knight, cover, 5,
Tamara Kulikova, 6, Zino, 1, 10

Printed in the United States of America in North Mankato, Minnesota.
122011   006498R

TABLE OF CONTENTS

A *Magical* World

The best poems are magical, miniature worlds.

When you read a poem, you might step into a crowded market, a football field, or a slow-rolling river. The smell of garlic or firecrackers may fill the air. Nearby you might see a giraffe or a circus acrobat. Or maybe you even become one of those characters. A great poem is like a short vacation to an exotic land.

Creating this fascinating world can be tricky. Sometimes you're just not sure what to put in your poem.

That's where photos can help. A good photo is like a grab bag. It's full of specific items, sounds, colors, scenes, characters, and moods. Grab whatever you want from the photo, and use those elements in your poem!

A great photo will have your mind overflowing with ideas. Let the following writing exercises prove it to you. The power of photos will be as plain as the ladybug on your face.

The writing Process

Step 1 Prewrite

Plan what you're going to write. Are you going to write a fiction story, a poem, or some other form of writing? Choose a topic, and start brainstorming details. Also identify your audience and the purpose of your piece.

Step 2 Draft

Put your ideas on paper. Start crafting your composition. Don't worry about getting the punctuation and grammar perfect. Just start writing.

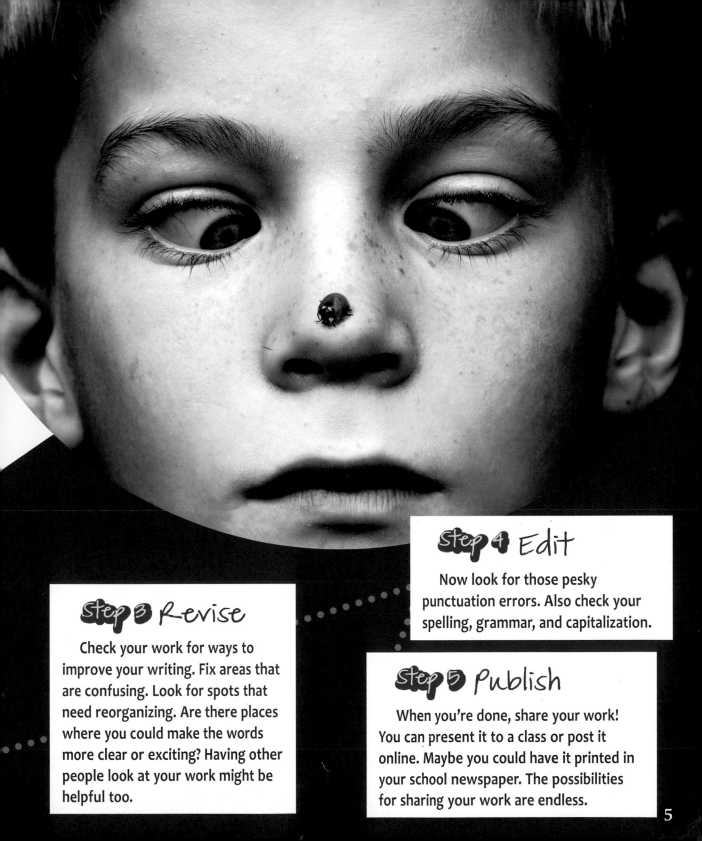

Step 3 Revise

Check your work for ways to improve your writing. Fix areas that are confusing. Look for spots that need reorganizing. Are there places where you could make the words more clear or exciting? Having other people look at your work might be helpful too.

Step 4 Edit

Now look for those pesky punctuation errors. Also check your spelling, grammar, and capitalization.

Step 5 Publish

When you're done, share your work! You can present it to a class or post it online. Maybe you could have it printed in your school newspaper. The possibilities for sharing your work are endless.

5

Chapter 1

IDEAS, IMAGES, AND METAPHOR

Poem Topics

Do you have trouble finding poetry ideas?

Well, every photo is an idea factory. What comes to mind when you look at this image of wild socks and shoes?

Do you think of:

- the Wicked Witch from *The Wizard of Oz*?

- striped prison uniforms?

- when your sister threw up at her dance recital?

- shoe shopping with your mom?

You could write a poem about any of these ideas. Your poem might not directly describe the picture, but that's OK. Images are just tools to get your brain going.

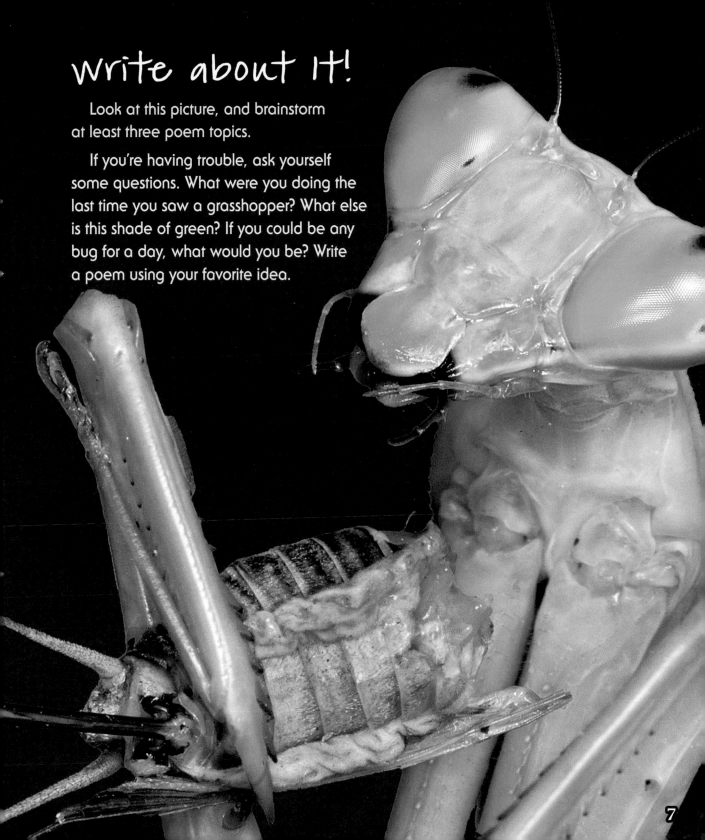

write about It!

Look at this picture, and brainstorm at least three poem topics.

If you're having trouble, ask yourself some questions. What were you doing the last time you saw a grasshopper? What else is this shade of green? If you could be any bug for a day, what would you be? Write a poem using your favorite idea.

Sensory Details

Fantastic poems don't just tell about a scene. They make you feel like you're actually there.

Sensory details give readers sights, sounds, tastes, textures, and smells. Details draw readers into the poet's world. You can discover those delicious details in photos.

Imagine you're on this tank in the desert. Notice the dusty plants and the red ground. Listen to the gunfire and foreign voices. Smell the gunpowder and sweat.

Practice finding details by creating a sensory chart. Put five columns on a sheet of paper. Label the columns see, hear, smell, taste, and touch. Look at a photo, and brainstorm words for each column. Then use words from your list to make a **vivid**, lively poem. Here's a poem inspired by this photo and a sensory chart.

Waiting

Dust cakes his lips

He tastes salt and heat

as he rolls through the dry, orange sea

Commands crackle in his ear

He swivels, alert—

Will a boom rattle his tank, shake the desert?

sensory—to do with the five senses
vivid—sharp and clear

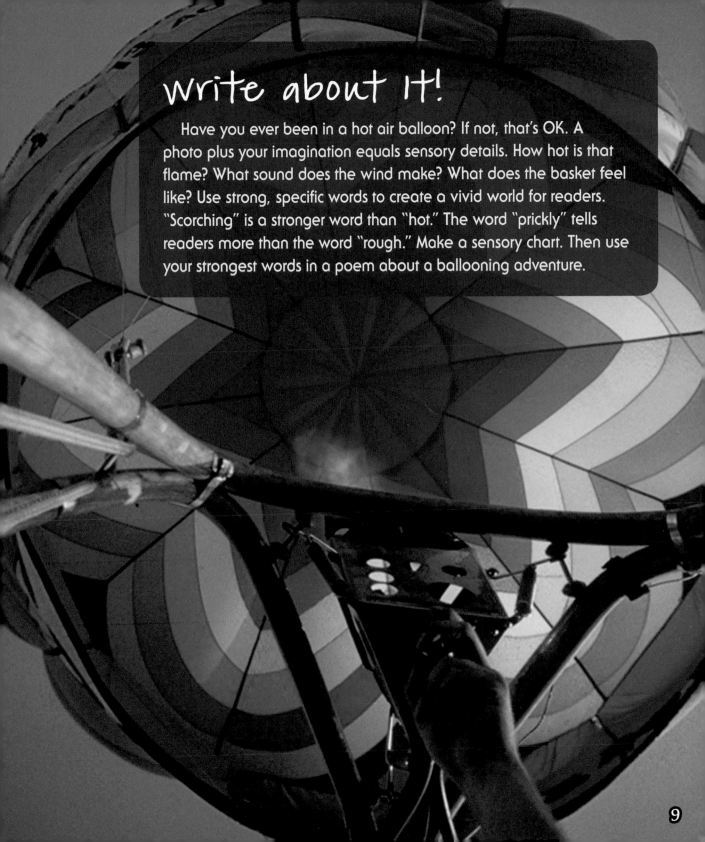

write about It!

Have you ever been in a hot air balloon? If not, that's OK. A photo plus your imagination equals sensory details. How hot is that flame? What sound does the wind make? What does the basket feel like? Use strong, specific words to create a vivid world for readers. "Scorching" is a stronger word than "hot." The word "prickly" tells readers more than the word "rough." Make a sensory chart. Then use your strongest words in a poem about a ballooning adventure.

Making Metaphors

Poets often describe things in unusual ways by using **metaphors**. Metaphors compare two unlike things, like a hose and a snake. Photos can really help you see how one object is similar to another. What ideas pop up when you look at this frosty window? Maybe you see feathers, flowers, and hearts. You could use all of these ideas in a poem.

Night Garden

Jack Frost planted flowers
on my window last night.

They bloomed at dawn, and doves
swooped down in a rush of icy white.

Their feathers etched valentines
in the glass before they flew away.

You can also choose just one comparison for a whole poem. This row of teeth could be a very dangerous necklace.

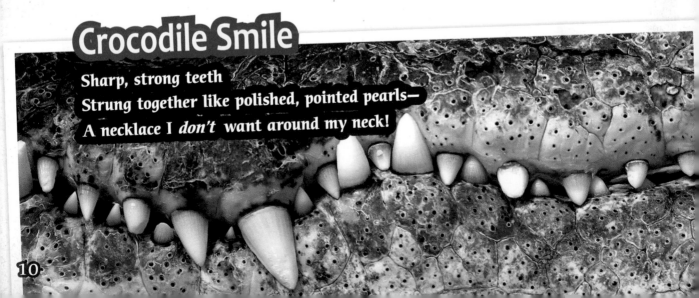

Crocodile Smile

Sharp, strong teeth
Strung together like polished, pointed pearls—
A necklace I *don't* want around my neck!

write about it!

Great poetry uses descriptions that make readers stop and think. Try to describe this fireworks display in an unusual way. Look past the bright lights and dazzling colors. Can you spot the shape of some other object? Now write a poem comparing these fireworks to something else.

metaphor—a way to describe something by calling it something else

Chapter 2

WORD CHOICES

Emotional Nouns

Poems are great for expressing emotions. But just saying your puppy makes you happy doesn't help readers feel your joy. Instead, fill your poem with descriptive **concrete nouns** that help readers identify with the scene and the emotion. Where can you find concrete nouns?

Look at a photo. Brainstorm nouns that describe the scene. This photo of destruction brings to mind nouns such as tornado, funnel, teddy bear, splinters, roof, floor, ground, and dirt. In a poem, concrete nouns clearly describe the scene and the emotion without using the word "sad."

After the Tornado

Spinning funnel

Thundered through town

Now there's a roof on the ground

Floorboards are torn like splintered bones

Teddy bear lies in the dirt, alone

concrete noun—a specific person, place, or thing that vividly points to a particular item

moody Verbs

Another way to strengthen a poem is through mood. **Verbs** that convey a mood help pump up the power of a poem.

Look at the desert image. It has no obvious mood or emotion. So pick any mood such as joyful, dangerous, or lonely. As you look at the image, try to feel that emotion. Then brainstorm strong verbs that relate to that emotion.

Verbs that might show anger include poke, glare, shove, crawl, slither, and shout. Use strong verbs like these to create a moody poem about the image.

Shouting at the Sky

One stiff flower
shoves above the rest,

Stomps on
glaring grasses.

It shouts at the sky,
until even

Its shadow
slithers away.

verb—an action word

14

write about It!

This classroom photo has no obvious mood. Just pick one! You could write about the joy of the final bell. Or a custodian's disgust at a messy floor. Or the loneliness of the empty chairs. Brainstorm strong verbs. Then use those verbs in a powerful poem. For an extra challenge, ask someone else to choose the mood for your poem.

unexpected words

Memorable poems often contain unexpected words.

The phrase "liquid moon" in a poem is unexpected. The moon isn't liquid. But if the poem describes night as soft and dreamy, liquid fits right in. Try surprising yourself and your readers by working a **random** word or phrase into your poem.

TO START, USE A PICTURE TO INSPIRE A FIRST DRAFT.

TiGER SNARLS,
WANTS TO ATTACK—
POUNCES ON ME

Then open any book. Without looking, put your finger on a word. Figure out how that word relates to the picture. Then revise your first draft to include that random word. The random word for this tiger poem was "**GOOD**."

IT TOOK THE POEM IN A WHOLE NEW DIRECTION!

TiGER SNARLS,
POUNCES ON ME.
GOOD JOB,
PURRS THE MOTHER TiGER.

random—without any plan or method

write about It!

Pretend you're on this roller coaster. What emotion do you feel? Now brainstorm concrete nouns and mood-setting verbs. What can you see? What do you hear? Write a poem using your strongest words. Then work in a random word. This word will add that unexpected, surprising element to your poem.

Filler Words

Imagery, action, and mood are the key ingredients in a poem.

Often, lazy filler words that don't add action or mood sneak into first drafts. That's no problem. Just get rid of them when you revise. Here are just a few filler words to beware of:

- the
- of
- really
- because
- **that**
- and

Instead of fillers, pack in concrete nouns and vivid verbs to make your poem strong. This task is doubly important in a short poetic form such as haiku.

Haiku poems usually capture single moments in nature. Each haiku has just 17 syllables and three lines. The lines follow a pattern of five, seven, then five syllables. Poems that short have no room for filler words.

Since every photo captures a moment, a photo is like a picture haiku. This photo of a maple tree and snow brings to mind many vivid and seasonal words. What strong words do you like in this haiku?

WHITE SNOW, SCARLET LEAVES
FLAKE BY LIGHT, DELICATE FLAKE—
WINTER BURIES FIRE

write about It!

Check out this crocodile hatching. Write a haiku that captures this moment. Try to be as specific as you can. Don't just describe hatching. Tell readers about *this* animal, *this* egg, *this* day, *this* moment. All in 17 syllables!

imagery—descriptive language that creates a picture for readers

Chapter 3

CHARACTERS

who are You?

Poems have characters just like novels do. Sometimes characters feel like real people you could hang out with.

A **first-person** poem is a great way to write about a character. When writing a first-person poem, you write as if you are the character.

Imagine you're the worker in this photo. Why did you choose this job? Are you afraid of heights? Who are you thinking about? Your answers will build a character.

Writing first-person poems lets you see the world through other people's eyes. You have to think about the words and phrases they would use. Their **voice** might be very different from yours. In fact, that's what makes first-person writing fun! It's a chance to imagine another life for a little while.

first person—telling a story from a personal viewpoint, using the words "I" or "we"
voice—the way a person speaks and thinks

write about It!

Imagine you're this skater. How do you feel? Are you scared or excited? Or perhaps you're annoyed that a certain person isn't watching. Decide what you, as this skater, want to write about. Then draft a poem using first-person words. Here are just a few first-person words to get you going—I, me, and my.

unusual characters

CAN A CAVE BE A CHARACTER?
IT CAN—IN A MASK POEM.

A mask poem is a first-person poem written in an object's voice. With a mask poem, you'll create a **personality** for a nonliving object. These kinds of poems surprise readers by creating a new side to an ordinary thing.

For this picture, you could write from the **point of view** of the sea cave, the ocean, or even the single wave. Start by looking at the image and deciding which object you will become. Then ask some questions:

What am I thinking?
How do I feel?
What do I want to happen?

Then draft a poem based on one of your answers. You can give your object any personality or abilities you want. For example, it's fun to compare a crashing wave to the spit of a person's sneeze.

SEA CAVE

I OPEN
MY ROCKY
MOUTH WIDE
AND SNEEZE
OUT THE
SEA—AH-CHOO!

write about It!

Study this drop of water. Imagine you are the droplet. You're falling, falling, falling. What does it feel like to be a falling water droplet? Do you dread being gargled or flushed? Be the water, and write a mask poem to share your personality.

personality—the traits that make one person different from others

point of view—the way someone or something looks at or thinks about something

Chapter 4

ARRANGING WORDS ON A PAGE

Free Verse

A poem's words are important, but so is the way a poem looks. A poem's arrangement gives readers clues about how it should be read. Free verse poems don't rhyme and have no clear line endings. So you can arrange the lines any way you want.

Here are a few tips:

- **Line breaks**—If you end a line midthought, readers will hurry to the next line. End a line with a complete thought, and readers will pause.

- **White space**—An overcrowded page can feel busy, like the beehive photo. Use spacing to make your poem focused and clear.

- **Line length**—Several long lines in a row make readers speed up. Then a very short line makes them slow down and focus.

Most importantly, you should like the way your poem looks on the page. Here's one poem, two ways.

Digging for Treasure

there's gold overhead and gold on my back, but the real gold is under my wings, buried deep, powdered gems that stick to my feet while I'm sipping on dreams and dancing in pollen

or

Digging for Treasure

there's gold overhead
and gold on my back,

but the real gold
is under my wings,

buried deep,
powdered gems that stick to my feet

while I'm sipping on dreams and
dancing in pollen

write about It!

Write a free verse poem inspired by these ballroom dancers. Then try playing with the line breaks. Keep the words the same, but change the way they look on the page. Ask a friend to read the different versions of your poem out loud. Which reading matches how you want the poem to sound?

Concrete Poems

Readers won't usually see the photos that inspire your poems. But with a concrete poem, you create a poem that is an image. This photo of a woman playing piano brings a couple of shapes to mind—music notes and piano keys. You could form a poem about music into one of those shapes. In a concrete poem, the poem's shape should relate to its topic. A poem shaped like piano keys that describes your lunch would confuse readers!

MUSIC FROM MY MIND DANCES AND SPINS AND FLOWS LIKE A BREEZE BUT MUSIC FROM MY FINGERS ALWAYS FALLS FLATFLATFLATFLATFLATFLATFLATFLATFLATFLATFLATFLAT

Do you create your poems on a computer?

If so, be ready for the challenge of concrete poems. Sketch your poem on paper first to figure out its general shape. Then play around with fonts and shapes in a word processing or image editing program. It might take a few tries to get the words in just the right shape.

write about It!

Images of night scenes can suggest many different shapes. Study this photo. What comes to mind for you? Write a poem inspired by this image. Then play with your poem's shape. You're not just creating a picture in readers' minds—you're making a picture!

Your Inspiration Toolkit

Photos are powerful tools that can help strengthen your poems. They can inspire emotion or speak to your senses. They can even help you look at an object in a new way.

Take a look at a cathedral or a painting. You don't see the hammer or brush that made them. You only see the finished pieces. People who read your poems probably won't see the photos you use for inspiration. But images are important tools that help you build great poems. How will photos inspire you?

write about It!

Look at the gargoyle guarding this building. Study his slumped stone posture. What is he thinking about so deeply? Brainstorm ideas about what this picture makes you think of. Feel the emotion in the picture and in yourself. Then grab a pen or a keyboard ... and write!

GLOSSARY

concrete noun (KON-kreet NOUN)—a specific person, place, or thing that vividly points to a particular item; the word dog is a general noun, while poodle is a concrete noun

first person (FURST PER-suhn)—telling a story from a personal viewpoint; first-person writing uses personal words such as I, me, and we

imagery (IM-ij-ree)—descriptive language that creates a picture in a poem or story

metaphor (MET-uh-for)—a way of describing something by calling it something else

personality (pur-suh-NAL-uh-tee)—the qualities that make one person different from others

point of view (POINT UV VYOO)—the way someone or something looks at or thinks about something

random (RAN-duhm)—without any order or purpose

sensory (SEN-suh-ree)—having to do with the five senses

verb (VURB)—a word that expresses an action

vivid (VIV-id)—sharp and clear

voice (VOISS)—the speech and thoughts of a character

READ MORE

Magee, Wes. *How to Write Poems.* How to Write. Laguna Hills, Calif.: QEB Pub., 2007.

Minden, Cecelia, and Kate Roth. *How to Write a Poem.* Language Arts Explorer Junior. Ann Arbor, Mich.: Cherry Lake Pub., 2011.

Salas, Laura Purdie. *Write Your Own Poetry.* Write Your Own. Minneapolis: Compass Point Books, 2008.

INTERNET SITES

FactHound offers a safe, fun way to find Internet sites related to this book. All of the sites on FactHound have been researched by our staff.

Here's all you do:

Visit *www.facthound.com*

Type in this code: 9781429661249

Super-cool stuff! Check out projects, games and lots more at
www.capstonekids.com

INDEX

ABOUT THE AUTHOR

Laura Purdie Salas is the author of more than 80 poetry and nonfiction books for kids and teens. Her titles include *Stampede! Poems to Celebrate the Wild Side of School* (a Minnesota Book Award finalist) and *Shrinking Days, Frosty Nights: Poems about Fall*. She loves to introduce kids and poetry to each other. Laura also loves reading, racquetball, school visits, Rock Band, and board games.